COUNTRIES, REGIONAL STUDIES, TRADING BLOCKS, UNIONS, WORLD ORGANIZATIONS

THE COSTS OF LAND REGISTRATION IN GHANA

COUNTRIES, REGIONAL STUDIES, TRADING BLOCKS, UNIONS, WORLD ORGANIZATIONS

Additional books in this series can be found on Nova's website under the Series tab.

Additional E-books in this series can be found on Nova's website under the E-books tab.

COUNTRIES, REGIONAL STUDIES, TRADING BLOCKS, UNIONS, WORLD ORGANIZATIONS

THE COSTS OF LAND REGISTRATION IN GHANA

FELIX N. HAMMOND
AND
RAYMOND T. ABDULAI

Nova Science Publishers, Inc.
New York

For permission to use material from this book please contact us:
Telephone 631-231-7269; Fax 631-231-8175
Web Site: http://www.novapublishers.com

Additional color graphics may be available in the e-book version of this book.

LIBRARY OF CONGRESS CATALOGING-IN-PUBLICATION DATA
Hammond, Felix N.
The costs of land registration in Ghana / Felix N. Hammond, Raymond T. Abdulai.
p. cm.
ISBN 978-1-61728-959-0 (softcover)
1. Land use--Ghana. 2. Land titles--Registration and transfer--Ghana. I. Abdulai, Raymond T. II. Title.
HD1022.Z63H36 2010
346.66704'38--dc22
2010026194

Published by Nova Science Publishers, Inc. † New York

CONTENTS

PREFACE

Real estate is so important a subject that it cannot be left out any serious macroeconomic deliberation and the collective quest for investment, wealth creation, poverty alleviation and economic development. This is amply demonstrated by the negative effects that the current real estate market downturn is having on every facet of the economies of rich nations. The role played by, especially, private real estate in the economic development of the advanced world is well documented. The importance of well established real estate markets that operate efficiently cannot, therefore, be over-emphasised. One area that has and continues to dominate discussions relates to how real estate market information should be organized and managed to guide participants in the markets to make efficient purchase, sale and investment decisions. It is often the responsibility of the stateto organize and manage real estate market information through implementation of land registration programmes. In Ghana, despite 126 years of unbroken history of implementing land registration programmes, it is estimated that only 8% of real estate ownership has been registered. It is important to properly comprehend this problem and its fundamental causes in order to proffer the appropriate remedies. Using the quantitative research methodology, this study seeks to offer explanations of the large lag in land registration in Ghana. It has been established that the fundamental root cause of the problem is the fact that the operation of Ghanaian state agencies that are responsible for the organization, management and dissemination of real estate market information is not based on clear economic principles. As a starting point, it is recommended that a nationwide timed-bound real estate ownership census akin to the survey conducted in Britain that resulted in the Domesday Book of 1086 be carried out and it should be financed by the government. From then onwards, it should be in the interest of the state to ensure that every real estate ownership or transaction is recorded by instituting an incentive package that would attract people to register; after all, such information would be sold to the public at a price. In this way a viable real estate ownership information system would be created, which would enable the real estate market to operate efficiently.

Chapter 1

INTRODUCTION

That real estate is so important a subject to be left out of consideration in any serious macroeconomic deliberation and in the collective quest for investment, wealth creation, poverty alleviation and economic development is amply attested to by the current downturn in real estate markets across the developed world (Abdulai and Hammond, 2008). Economic historians like North and Thomas (1973), Rosenberg and Birdzell (1986), Torstensson (1994) and Goldsmith (1995) have documented the role played by, particularly, private real estate in the economic development of advanced nations. Indeed, shelter and for that matter real estate, has been and continues to be one of the major global economic drivers. Housing, for instance, has played a major role in shaping the business cycles of countries like USA, Britain, New Zealand and Canada (Hale, 2008). According Hale (2008), from 2000-2005, for instance, house prices rose by 78% in Australia, 65% in New Zealand, 50% in Canada, 102% in Britain and 50% in the USA and this housing boom within the period produced negative savings rates and higher consumer spending in such countries. Hale (2008) further observes that the current weakness in house prices caused by the credit crunch has produced a downturn in consumer spending especially in Britain and the USA. In Britain alone, currently, there are 11.8 million residential mortgages, with loans worth over £1.2 trillion (CML, 2008) and the commercial real estate markets alone contribute some 6% to its annual Gross Domestic Product (GDP) (BPF, 2006). The figure is bound to be considerably more if the contributions of residential and other segments of the real estate market are taken into account in Britain.

The above shows that there is a connection between real estate and economic development. It, therefore, implies that the performance of any economy is, to a large extent, contingent upon the performance of its underlying real estate markets. This point is self-evident across the rich countries of the world but as aptly noted by Hammond (2006), it is less so in developing nations, particularly in sub-Saharan Africa. It follows that, if correctly organised, real estate markets in developing countries, particularly, in sub-Saharan Africa, could spur greater economic growth and possibly facilitate the lifting of the four-fifth of the regions population that currently survive on less than US$2.50 a day (Chen and Ravallion, 2008).

In order to attain these ends, real estate markets must facilitate large volumes of year-on-year first time and repeat voluntary real estate trades. It must also interact constructively with the financial system to facilitate large volumes of year-on-year real estate based credit transactions and indirect investments in real estate. By fostering large volumes of first time and repeat transactions in real estate, especially, between well informed voluntary buyers, sellers, borrowers and creditors, real estate markets are able to continually push real estate resources from lower productive uses to higher productive uses. By so doing, they ensure that real estate in a given society continually improves upon its contributions to the economic development processes.

The trouble is real estate markets are typically beset with fundamental restraints, which prevent or slow down the conduct of large volume of first time and repeat real estate trades. These restraints generally consist of ill-defined property rights (Alchian, 1965; Demsetz, 1967; Pejovich, 1990; Feder and Feeney, 1991), high transaction costs (Coase, 1960; Williamson, 1981; Rao, 2003), monopolisation of segments of the real estate markets, uncontrolled negative side effects of libertarian competition and the possible non-provision of public goods (Smith, 1776; Hicks, 1939; Harberger, 1959; Friedman, 2002). Whilst all of these restraints are important and need urgent attention, costly access to full and perfect information is lately being recognised as the most enduring restraint (Stigler, 1961; Williamson, 1991; Wyatt & Fisher, 1998; Rose, 2002), especially, in less developed economies. To appreciate the reasons why costly and imperfect information is critical, it is important to commence with the nature and purpose of the real estate markets.

Most real estate trades involve the reciprocal interchange of property rights on one hand and money on the other. In effect, through trade, the parties interchange positions – the original owner of the real estate takes the place of the original owner of the price money and vice versa. Thereafter, the new owner of the real estate gains the backing of the law to make whatever uses and profits from the real estate, subject of course to the provisions of land use planning and other relevant laws of the society. The new owner may use the real estate as collateral to raise capital for investments to earn better returns. At the same time, the law disables all others from making any use or decisions regarding the real estate unless where the law so permits. The economic view is that buyers pay a price to interchange positions with original owners because, in their estimation, the original owners have undervalued or underpriced the economic potentials of the real estate in so far as its future rents/benefits are concerned (Smith, 1776). Likewise, the owners of real estate may also feel that purchasers have undervalued the real worth or benefits of the money they intend to use in purchasing it and that they (the owners of the real estate) can generate more returns from the money than anticipated by the purchasers.

Consequently, by interchanging positions, buyers are able to make such uses of the real estate involved or rearrange or modify it in a manner that will enable it to generate the anticipated full benefits. Buyers who are proven right by the coming market events reap better benefits/returns from the real estate than what the original owners would have reaped. By buying, improving and putting real estate to those uses that generate higher benefits/returns, purchasers, through the interchange, push the real estate from lower productive uses to higher productive uses. If real estate that was the subject matter of a previous transaction is subsequently sold again, all things being equal, it would be pushed further into a higher productive use and so on. By so doing, real estate continually increases its contributions to the economic development processes.

Real estate markets function well when buyers, creditors, investors, sellers, borrowers and issuers make informed decisions and choices relating to sales, purchases and pricing. The ability of actors to make informed decisions depends on easy and cheap access to high quality and clear information on which they make their decisions. To aid this, there is the need for real estate market participants to possess upfront, clear and quality information on all available real estate stock on the market at any given time. They must also know the true owners of each available stock. Finally, they must have information relating to recent transactions involving comparable real estate.

Without such upfront information, transacting parties will suffer from information deficit with severe consequences. Firstly, purchasers or investors suffering from information deficit may end up paying more for real estate than the total income that it is capable of generating. Likewise, creditors may end up advancing more credit than the economic worth of the real estate in question. Secondly, since the essence of the transaction is for the parties to interchange positions, purchasers or creditors may end up paying the price money or advancing credit to phony owners. This is very crucial, because, without buying the property rights from the actual owner, the law will disable the buyer, creditor or investor from taking the place of the true owner. Thus, if the purported seller is not actually the owner, the buyer, by paying the seller, misallocates his or her financial resources. As always, the market will punish such misallocations with economic loses. Such buyers, creditors and investors will, as a result, lose their money and gain nothing in return. It is a rational expectation that buyers, creditors and investors would seek keenly to avoid or minimise such punishments. They will, thus, strive to feel sure that the purported sellers they intend to deal with are, indeed, the undisputed owners, before embarking on the transactions.

However, without a workable system to provide the key information at the right quality, with the right contents, in the right form and at reasonable cost, there is a real risk that real estate market participants may make their most serious decisions based on suspicious data and many would end up as recipients of the punishments of the market. The cost of information deficit can be huge, though less readily obvious. These costs include loss of money through payments to phony parties, ownership litigation expenses, loss of income earning opportunities and so on. The prospects of such cost would lower the confidence of market participants, thereby slowing down the rate of transactions, which will in turn slow down the performance of the market and hence deny the development process of the invaluable contributions that the real estate market could have made to it.

Fortunately, real estate is an example of search goods (Hammond, 2006; Abdulai, 2007) and hence distinct from experience goods such as a meal. Unlike experience goods whose potential benefits can only be ascertained after consumption, it is possible to search and discover sufficient information about real estate far before they are purchased or admitted as collateral in credit transactions (Weiner and Vining, 1999; Hammond, 2006). It is possible, for instance, to discover through inspections the relevant information regarding its essential physical (for example size, location and neighbourhood quality), legal (property rights and restrictions) and economic (price and rental values) attributes that determine its utilities before arriving at a final purchase or price decisions. The implications are three-fold.

Firstly, in an economic system in which the requisite information is readily available at zero search cost, owners (borrowers) or sellers (creditors) would base their purchase, sale or price decisions on concrete and reliable information or market data. This will expectedly lead to optimal decisions on price and quantities that "will satisfy preference to the greatest extent possible" (Nell, 1984). Secondly, where, on the other hand, because of its technical nature, the data is not intelligible to the market participants above, they may seek advice from those equipped with the skills and expertise in analysing such data. These specialists may include valuers, lawyers and estate agents. Thirdly, where the required information is non-existent, severely disorganised, out of date or considerably costly to obtain, market participants as well as market intermediaries such as valuers, estate agents and lawyers may end up basing purchase, sale or pricing decisions on suspicious or severely inadequate information.

By its very nature, however, most of the information that buyers could base their decisions on are held by the owners of the real estate. Meanwhile because real estate transactions are not contracts of good faith (Uberrimae Fidei), owners are not under legal obligations to disclose any information known to them, which could help buyers form their views on the terms of trade. Besides, the prospects of opportunistic behaviours suggest that buyers cannot fully trust the information volunteered by owners as they could be inaccurate or intended to mislead them. The alternative will be for buyers to conduct their own private real estate research and interviews with neighbours to procure the relevant information needed for their decisions. This, however, is time consuming and a costly process. As Stigler (1961), Vickrey (1961) and Mirrlees (1971) argue, because of the cost involved in information gathering, actors are inevitably less than fully informed when they make their most optimal market decisions.

Traditionally, buyers rely on publicly accessible information systems such as land registration and cadastral systems to develop their views as to the validity of the claims of ownership made by the parties purporting to sell or use the real estate as security in credit transactions. In the case of Ghana, however, the World Bank (2007) estimates that these publicly available systems hold just about 8% of information on real estate transactions. Thus, there are about nine in ten chances that information on real estate that a buyer is interested in would not be held in these systems. This makes buyers to incur high costs to investigate the true ownership position privately through market inquiries and interviews with neighbours. This heightens the cost of real estate transactions in Ghana, which may be slowing down the development of its real estate market. It is the job of government to alleviate these costs to get the market operating at efficient levels. To do this, there is the need, first, to understand the causes of the considerable backlog of real estate ownership information capture and through the causation proffer workable solutions. It is this aim the chapter seeks to pursue.

The rest of the chapter is organised as follows. The section that follows this introduction describes the land registration systems that exist globally after which section three gives an overview of the Ghanaian land registration systems. The research methodology adopted for the study is described in section four whilst section five presents and discusses the date collected from a field survey. The penultimate section deals with implications and the last section concludes the chapter.

Chapter 2

LAND REGISTRATION

TYPES OF LAND REGISTRATION SYSTEMS

Globally there are two types of land registration systems, which are deed registration and title registration. The fundamental principles that underpin the two systems are explicated as follows. In a deed registration system, legally recognized and protected real estate ownership arises upon conclusion of an agreement or contract between the real estate grantor and grantee (Deininger, 2003). According to Deininger (2003), the entry of the agreement and its key contents into the public registry is to provide notice to the world of the existence of the real estate ownership and challenges to it will be handled through civil litigation. However, in a title registration system, it is the entry into the registry that gives the ownership legal validity, guaranteed by the State; all entries in the register are *prima facie* evidence of the legal status of the real estate (Deininger, 2003).

Even though in the title registration system, legal validity of real estate ownership arises from the fact of registration, it is important to note that it does not emanate from only registration. In the deed registration system, for example, legal validity arises from the contract or agreement between the grantor and grantee and not from registration. Furthermore, legal validity and recognition of real estate ownership can emanate from other legislation apart from the title registration system depending on the legal system that operates in a particular country. In Ghana, for example, the customary or traditional system of real estate ownership is not based on registration but it is recognized by the legal system. Under Ghana's customary law, proof of real estate ownership is not by any form of documentation; it is rather by physical occupation and possession and the recognition of this fact by members of the society, particularly, adjoining owners of real estate (Antwi, 2000; Abdulai, 2006 and 2007). However, under the 1992 Constitution of Ghana (the supreme law of the country) and the Conveyancing Decree of 1973 (NRCD 175), the customary system of real estate ownership is recognized by the common law courts. Indeed, legal recognition of Ghana's customary system of real estate ownership dates back to 1925 when the British colonial administrators introduced the Native Courts (Crook, 2002).

In Nigeria, despite the nationalization of land under the Land Use Decree of 1978, customary real estate transactions (which are not based on any form of documentation) are recognized by the state sponsored court system in so far as they are consistent with existing State law and are also not opposed to public policy (Ikejiofor, 2006). Other countries in the developing world where the customary system of real estate ownership is legally recognised (whether it is registered or not) include Mozambique, Lesotho, Malawi, Mali, Namibia, Niger, South Africa, Swaziland, Tanzania, Uganda, Zambia and Zimbabwe (Alden-Wiley, 2002; cited in Deininger, 2003). Unregistered real estate ownership is legally recognised in the United Kingdom; however, in unregistered real estate sales, the law requires the root of title to be investigated 15 years back (which used to be 30 years per-dating 1970) before the trading takes place (Abdulai, 2006; MacKenzie and Phillips, 2008).

In comparative terms, the gap between the percentage of real estate ownership that is registered in the developing and developed world is very huge. Available data from de Soto (2000), Deininger (2003), World Bank (2007), Abdulai (2007) and HM Land Registry (2009) bespeak that in the developing world, the percentage of registered real estate ownership is 15 whilst in the advanced world, it ranges from 65% to 100%. In Africa, it is 2% - 10% while in East Asia it is less than 30%.

Having distinguished between the types of land registration systems that exist globally, it is expedient at this stage to explain how real estate and its registration affect the economic development of a nation. It is real estate that is normally accepted by financial institutions as collateral for advancing loans for investment. Real estate is regarded as a suitable collateral asset because it is a commodity that is consumed in situ; that is, it is an immovable asset. The importance of mort-gaging one's real estate asset to financial institutions cannot be over-emphasised from the perspective of both the mortgagor (borrower) and the mortgagee (lender). This is because collateral arrangements partly or fully shift the risks of loan loss from the mortgagee to the mortgagor. In the event of default on the part of the mortgagor, it will trigger the loss of his or her mortgaged real estate. Thus, for the mortgagee, the collateral provides a form of protection or insurance against the loss of the loan since there are normally enough legal arrangements to foreclose the mortgage transaction where the mortgagor defaults. At the same time, the prospect of losing one's real estate is an incentive for the mortgagor to be committed regarding the repayment of the loan granted.

The pledging of real estate, accompanied by the registration of ownership and mortgage transactions tremendously overcomes the problems of asymmetrical information and moral hazard. Land registration is a record keeping system and, therefore, creates a real estate ownership database, which is very important in every economy. When information is recorded in a central system, which is accessible to the public, it makes it easy for such data to be accessed for various purposes. The availability of a real estate ownership database facilitates real estate transactions and real estate taxation, which reduces transactions costs. De Soto (2000) alludes to this purpose when he emphasises the role of land registration in facilitating communication, information sharing, networking and transactions. In the absence of land registration, legal experts are often commissioned to conduct searches to trace the root of title in real estate transactions and verify that the real estate is not subject to any undisclosed obligations, which is normally a long process, time consuming and expensive. This point is amply demonstrated by what obtains in the UK and France. As earlier, indicated, in the UK where real estate is not registered and it is to be traded, the law requires that the root of title be investigated 15 years back. In the case of France, it is 30 years. Thus, land registration significantly enhances the smooth operation of real estate markets.

Regarding the registration of mortgages, the common law position is that if a mortgage transaction is not registered and the mortgagor clandestinely transfers the mortgaged real state via sale to a bona fide purchaser for value who is unaware of the existence of the mortgage transaction, the mortgage as an encumbrance will not be binding on such a purchaser (MacKenzie and Phillips, 2008). However, if the mortgage transaction is registered, the purchaser cannot defend himself or herself on the basis that he or she is a bona fide purchaser for value without notice since the existence of the mortgage will be a public record and based on the principle of caveat emptor, it will be his or her responsibility to check the public records. Thus, the registration of mortgage transactions protects lenders/financial institutions from the activities of unscrupulous mortgagors as it makes it impossible for any purchaser of mortgaged real estate to plead bona fide purchaser for value without notice. From the preceding discussion, it is obvious that real estate and land and mortgage registration play a critical role in the economic development of a nation; they greatly help to improve access to formal capital for investment and wealth creation.

REAL ESTATE OWNERSHIP INFORMATION SYSTEMS IN GHANA

Albeit traditionally, deeds and land title registration systems are the two main systems that have been employed by many nations to overcome real estate ownership information asymmetry, in Ghana, various parallel models of real estate ownership registration systems manned by six separate and independent public real estate sector institutions have emerged for the task. These are Lands Commission, Deed Registry, Land Title Registry, Survey Department, Land Valuation, Board, and Office of the Administrator of Stool Land[1] (OASL).

The earliest official real estate ownership registration system in the country is the deed registration system (manned by the Deed Registry which, is practically under Lands Commission), a legacy of the colonial order established largely to supposedly protect the interests of expatriate merchants of the colonial era (Meek, 1949). This commenced with the enactment of the Land Registry Ordinance (No. 8) in 1883, which was re-enacted in 1895 (cap 133) and revised in 1951. The first postcolonial administration, in 1962, replaced these laws with the Land Registry Act (Act 122), which made registration of instruments accompanied by a survey plan of the land, compulsory (Section 24 Act 122).

The second official though not juridical real estate ownership registration system is the Plotting System, which is manned by Lands Commission. This came into being when in 1945 the Stamp Ordinance (Cap 168) was amended (No. 29 of 1945) to introduce an internal administrative

[1] In Ghana, there are primarily two types of landownership, which are State and private landownership. Private land composes of traditional land (land vested in communities represented by chiefs/kings and families/clans) and individual land whilst State land refers to land that has been acquired by the State from the private land sector. In the southern part of Ghana, chiefs/kings as traditional rulers sit in state on specially designed stools or chairs. In the olden days, they sat in state on stools, which were regarded as the symbols of authority. However, as time progressed and with modernization, they started using specially designed chairs. Thus today, most of them use chairs but the stool remains the symbol of authority. In southern Ghana where land is vested in communities represented by chiefs/kings, it is call stool land whilst in northern Ghana, it is referred to as skin land.

requirement to attach a "Particulars Delivered Form" (PDF) to all real estate contract documents submitted to the erstwhile Lands Department (now Lands Commission) for the assessment and payment of stamp duty on the purchase or leasing of real estate. The PDF made provision for a short description of land and details of the transaction together with an annexed plan of the land and any building thereon. The extracts from these data together with the site plan was then plotted onto survey maps and referenced. This became an administrative parcel-based database in which data is organised around the proprietary land unit for valuation and stamp duty assessment purposes. Considering its purpose as an administrative database, which was not meant for public consumption, the scientific accuracy of the survey plans attached was not insisted on. Also as Brobbey (1991), a former chairman of Land Valuation Board (the original custodian of the system), states, consideration and prices stipulated in the transaction documents, which formed the basis and main inputs for this database were severely understated to evade higher stamp duty or tax liabilities.

Additionally, according to Antwi (2000), Hammond (2006) and Abdulai (2007), the plotting system admits irreconcilable data in respect of the same proprietary land unit, as that did not adversely affect the objective of the database. Yet, owing to the difficulties in obtaining search reports from the deed registration system as against the relative ease with which information could be obtained from the plotting system (because it was parcel-based), many real estate market participants relied more on unofficial searches from the plotting system as the basis for their real estate market decisions; at present about 90% of all real estate information searches are conducted from the plotting system instead of the juridical deed and land title registration systems even though the plotting registers still lack legal recognition (Hammond, 2006). Information obtained from this plotting system by the public confers no rights or obligations against the government regarding its accuracy. Records held in the plotting system are most of the time so inaccurate that invariably an inspection has to be conducted to confirm doubts in a majority of the cases submitted for registration; in some cases site visits have established that the real estate intended to be registered does not even exist on the geographical maps at all (Hammond, 2006).

The third model is the concurrence system, which is also handled by the Lands Commission. Practically the distinction between this system and the plotting system is only one of convenience. In 1962, the enactment of the Administration of Lands Act (Act 123) produced the curious outcome that non-commercial stool land transactions were not to be formalised and hence need not be captured within the prevailing official information machinery.

Transacting parties could, thus, dispense with the formalities of seeking the public recording of those transactions that are made "without payment of valuable consideration or in exchange for nominal consideration" (Act 123). Such transactions need not be evidenced in writing and need not be registered under the deed registry model as well as the plotting system. Under the same law, however, commercial stool land transactions that "involves the payment of any valuable consideration or which would, by reason of it being to a person not entitled by customary law to the free use of land involved the payment of any such consideration" (Section 8 of Act, 123) were to be compulsorily formalised. Since the deeds, plotting and concurrence systems are practically unified, the chapter will group them together in the ensuing analysis and discussion.

The fourth real estate ownership information system is the land title registration system, which was introduced in 1986 under the Land Title Registration Law of 1986 (PNDCL, 152). The law is currently operational in Greater Accra region and Kumasi in the Ashanti region only[2]. The agency responsible for title registration is the Land Title Registry. The system was introduced to replace the deeds registration model and by implication the plotting model as well. The implementation of the law had false starts with serious implications for the asymmetry problems. Firstly, an entirely new government department (the Land Title Registry) was established to carry out the implementation of the law. This engendered fierce clash of departmental interests as managers of the existing system felt their powers and influence were threatened by the new agency. The import of section 13 of the law was to ensure that within 90 days of declaring an area a registration district, all previously recorded transactions under the deeds system considered genuine and accurate were to be transferred directly onto the new land title register under PNDCL 152. Thereafter, deeds and plotting will cease to operate in the declared areas. However, to date (after almost 23 years) not a single document has been transferred this way. The practical consequences are that the land title system operates in parallel with the deeds and plotting systems. As aptly noted by Antwi (2000) and Hammond (2006), the harsh reality is that the information in these respective systems is not harmonised in any comprehensive way; indeed, often contradictory.

From the preceding discourse, it is obvious that government interventions in the area of real estate market information management in

[2] Ghana is divided into ten regions for political and administrative purposes and each region has a capital, which is the administrative centre. Greater Accra and Ashanti regions are some of the regions in Ghana. The capital of Greater Accra region is Accra, which is also the capital of Ghana and that of Ashanti region is Kumasi.

Ghana have had 126 years of unbroken history. Put roughly, for the registration systems to have been able to capture all existing real estate ownership or transactions information by now, assuming all information captured is accurate, the systems should have been capturing information at a rate of at least 0.8 percent (less then 1%) annually; this figure is calculated by simply dividing 100% coverage by the 126 years of land registration practice in Ghana. Yet according to AMCAD (1998), only about 30% of existing information on urban real estate has been captured as at 1998. This represents an information capture rate of about 0.26% per annum in urban areas of Ghana, which is about a third as fast as it should be. The World Bank finding referred to earlier that only 8% of information on real estate transactions across the country are recorded in the registration systems also indicates that a much slower national rate of capture than the 0.26% per annum. This implies that, even if all the information captured by these parallel registration systems is accurate and consistent (and they are not) only about 8% of the asymmetric information problems together with their economic repercussions would have been dealt with by these systems. The challenge to this chapter is to provide a convincing and empirically validated explanation to the large lag in real estate market information capture in Ghana and to offer practical solutions.

Chapter 3

RESEARCH METHODOLOGY

The quantitative, qualitative and mixed methodologies research approaches were examined as to their appropriateness for the study and the quantitative research methodology was finally adopted. Empirical data was collected in Ghana between June 2007 and January 2008 using field survey data collection procedures. The survey participants fell into two broad groups. The first group consisted of the government agencies in charge of the administration of the State real estate ownership information systems. The second group consisted of purchasers of real estate who had sought or were seeking to register their real estate ownership with the relevant systems.

With regard to the first group of survey participants, Lands Commission, Deeds and Land Title Registries represent the end points of all the activities directed at registration of real estate ownership in the country and were, therefore, the agencies surveyed. As earlier noted, the deeds, plotting and concurrence systems are practically unified and are, thus, grouped together under Lands Commission. Due to time and cost considerations, the study concentrated on Accra, which is the capital of Ghana; Accra also has the most active real estate market in the country. Data were obtained from these agencies through systematic records investigation and participant observation. Regarding participant observation, firstly, the chain link of activities involved in registering real estate ownership were meticulously observed individually, timed and costed. Each activity was observed and timed on three separate occasions without the prior notice of the observee. The average time for the three observations was then adopted as the typical time span for each activity.

Admittedly, the accuracy could have be improved if the number of observations had been increased, but prevailing time and cost constraints restricted the number of observations that could possibly be taken. Even so, this study is aimed at providing indications of the order of things and not to actually estimate pinpoint accurate figures. The average time per activity was then valued. The best way of valuing the time spent is to apply the time preference rate; that is, the going risk free interest rate (government bond rates), applicable at the time. However, government bond markets in Ghana are well known to be highly underdeveloped and overly laden with political influences to the extent that on occasions, the risk-free rate surpasses the risk adjusted rates obtainable from the country's stock market. It is, therefore, quite unreasonable to rely on the prevailing bond rates as accurate reflection of the time value of money in that country. Even if an accurate risk-free rate were obtainable, it has to be adjusted to reflect the risk of the activity by adding a risk premium to it. Being a public service, determining the applicable risk premium to apply is problematic and can be fraught with errors. As a result, the simplified way around this, was to adopt the average wage rate for the official performing the activity as the minimum time value of money rate. This is valid because, it at least, reflects the government's own (of course not the market) valuation of the time of the official. The time spent on an activity was, thus, multiplied by the wage rate of the official to arrive at the minimum estimate of the value of the activity.

Additionally, 303 real estate purchasers were randomly selected and surveyed using purposely-designed questionnaire administered face-to-face. No questionnaire was posted or left with respondents for later collection or administration. Generally, the questionnaire sought for data on how much it cost them in terms of time spent and out of pocket expenses to have their real estate ownership recorded in the public registers. Also, similar data on how much it cost to conduct a search from the registration systems was obtained from the respondents.

Chapter 4

Presentation of Data and Discussion

Delays

To ascertain whether the plotting/concurrence system is competent in capturing the relevant information early, fully and accurately, data on 235 randomly sampled documents supplied to the system and processed for concurrence under the concurrence and plotting systems were obtained. Table 1 shows the descriptive statistics on the times (in days) it took for the relevant property information to be captured into the concurrence information system.

The study identified a total of 22 bureaucratic steps in the information capture process and take, according to Table 1, 600 days on the average to complete the recording of information on an average plot size of 2.27 acres. Most of the documents were processed in 258 days (Mode). The fastest processing time was 34 days while the slowest processing time was 3,530 days. The crucial point at issue, however, is given that real estate transactions are occurring regularly in Ghana, the average processing time of 600 days means that the system could be some 600 days out of date at any particular time. The sluggishness of the system is clearly contributing significantly to the lag in information capture and even leading to the data available being possibly outdated.

The data used to analyze the speed of data capture under the land title registration system is the full data on applications made by real estate owners in the study area to the land title registry from the date of its inception in practice in 1988 to 2002 (15 years). The data, thus, represent the total return series for the 15-year period. The 2002 end point has been deliberately chosen because, in actual fact, the year 2002 marks a new era in land administration in Ghana. It is in reality the year that the ongoing Ghana Land Administration Project under the auspices of the World Bank took off in practice. The data and following analysis, therefore, provides an important baseline data against which the performance of the Ghana Land Administration project can be ascertained ex-post.

Table 2 provides statistical description of the data. According to the Table, on the average 7,452 applications are made to the Land Title Registry annually. Out of this, about 1,849 constituting 25% come from areas where pre-prepared sectional survey maps exist. Averagely 15.8 % of this (that is, the 25%) is completed per year, representing a backlog of about 84% per year of all applications coming from areas with pre-prepared sectional plans.

The cumulative effect of this 16% completion rate is extraordinary. Table 3 reports the data on the cumulative effects of annual backlogs imposed on succeeding years and then on the overall outstanding applications. The Table shows that over the period, the number of titles completed declined progressively to about 3% by 2002 of outstanding cases. The total backlog of cases as at 2002 stood at 94,106, representing about 97% of total requests for documentation, which could not be serviced.

To be able to make rational predictions about the processing time required to reduce the backlog considerably, an Ordinary Least Square (OLS) model is derived based on the data obtained. An additional independent dataset, *SECTPLAN* is included in the data contained in Table 3 to help estimate the impacts of the prior availability of sectional map for particular applications on the processing time. The key variables relied on in deriving the regression model are, thus, *YEAR* representing the year of applications, *APPLICATION*, representing the cumulative applications for particular years, *COMPLETED*, representing the number of applications completed in a particular year and *SECTPLAN* representing the number of applications for which sectional plans existed. For applications coming from areas where pre-prepared sectional maps exist, it is expected that the physical details of the proprietary land units were already known and the processing will not entail a re-survey of the land concerned.

The model summary from the regression analysis shows that the variables *SECTPLAN*, *APPLICATION* and *YEAR* as defined earlier explains about 65% (R Square = 0.646 in Table 4) of the number of titles completed in any particular year.

Table 5. Reports the regression coefficients of the model.

The results show that the functional relationship between the number of completed applications and the explanatory variables is:

Table 1. Descriptive Statistics on Processing Delays

	N	Minimum	Maximum	Mean		Mode	Std. Deviation
	Statistic	Statistic	Statistic	Statistic	Std. Error	Statistic	Statistic
Plot Size	235.00	0.01	61.42	2.27	0.59	0.32	9.00
Days	235.00	34.00	3530.00	599.90	41.50	258.00	636.19
Valid N (listwise)	235.00						

Source: Field Survey (2008).

Table 2. Descriptive Statistics

	N	Minimum	Maximum	Sum	Mean	Std. Deviation
Applications	15	2,274.00	23,409.00	11,1778.00	7,451.8667	5773.3847
Sectplan	15	172.00	24,59.00	27,731.00	1,848.7333	664.1310
Completed	15	150.00	2,663.00	17,672.00	1,178.1333	715.0598
Valid N (Listwise)	15					

Source: Field Survey (2008).

Table 3. Cumulative Delays in Land Title Registration

Year	Cumulative Pending Application	Completed	Backlog	% Completed
1988	2,274.00	843.00	1,431.00	37.07
1989	5,809.00	150.00	5,659.00	2.58
1990	11,318.00	400.00	10,918.00	3.53
1991	17,472.00	200.00	17,272.00	1.14
1992	29,120.00	1,010.00	28,110.00	3.47
1993	45,584.00	1,360.00	44,224.00	2.98
1994	67,633.00	2,000.00	65,633.00	2.96
1995	69,363.00	650.00	68,713.00	0.94
1996	74,563.00	1,906.00	72,657.00	2.56
1997	78,682.00	1,018.00	77,664.00	1.29
1998	83,494.00	1,977.00	81,517.00	2.37
1999	86,328.00	1,098.00	85,230.00	1.27
2000	89,677.00	1,147.00	88,530.00	1.28
2001	93,607.00	1,250.00	92,357.00	1.34
2002	96,769.00	2,663.00	94,106.00	2.75

Source: Field Survey, 2008.

Table 4. Correlation Coefficient

Model	R	R Square	Adjusted R Square	Std. Error of the Estimate
1	.804	.646	.549	480.1509

a Predictors: (Constant), SECTPLAN, APPLICATIONS, YEAR.

Table 5. Regression Coefficients

		Unstandardized Coefficients		Standardized Coefficients	t	Sig.
Model		B	Std. Error	Beta		
1	(Constant)	-300404.10	75629.66		-3.97	0.00
	Year	151.31	38.03	0.95	3.98	0.00
	Applications	0.08	0.03	0.63	2.68	0.02
	Sectplan	-0.46	0.29	-0.43	-1.60	0.14
a	Dependent Variable: Completed					

$$COMPLETED = -300404.10 + 151.31YEAR + 0.08APPLICATION - 0.46SECTIONPLAN$$

This indicates that the backlog situation increases or deteriorates by some 151 documents every year and the pre-existence of sectional maps helps improve the backlog situation only marginally by less than a day. The number of applications per particular year also contributes marginal increases to the existing backlog situation. What is perhaps more interesting is that, the number of completed applications in any given year is affected by the total number of applications submitted in the same year plus the hangover of incomplete applications from previous years. This is explained by the fact that, the backlog cases are not sitting unattended. Resources are allocated to work on them at various stages. But the limitation of resources means that the existing resources are so thinly spread out to cover all documents in the processing line that in the end only few are completed. The model predicts that, if things remain substantially unchanged, it would not be until the year 2070 that the backlogs could be cleared (61 years from 2009).

POLICY INDUCED ASYMMETRY

The land title registration and concurrence/plotting systems, as already noted, operate in parallel. Table 6 below reports the data on the documentation requests made to the respective systems between 1997 and 2002.

Table 6. Comparison of Documents Presented for Land Title Registration and Concurrence/Plotting Between 1997 and 2002

	2002	2001	2000	1999	1998	1997
Applications for plotting	6,861	14,371	9,229	6,610	4,858	4,267
Applications for land title registration	4,412.00	5,077.00	4,447.00	4,811.00	5,830.00	6,025.00
Difference	2,449.00	9,294.00	4,782.00	1,799.00	-972.00	-1,758.00

Source: Data on the applications for plotting was obtained from the records of the Lands Commission, Accra while the data on applications for land title registration was obtained from the records of the Land Title Registry, Accra.

According to the data, with the exception of 1997 and 1998, documentation requests made to the plotting system consistently outstripped those to the land title registration system. It is known in practice that some real estate owners who can afford prefer to direct their documentation requests to both systems. But not many do that, as it is costly. This has led, expectedly, to inconsistent dataset and even the prevalence of irreconcilable information on the same real estate held in the two systems. This is ironic given that the plotting system lacked legal recognition while the title registration system is legally compulsory, at least according to the enabling law. Clearly, there is a market signal in favour of the plotting system even though the signal is not strong enough to eliminate land title registration altogether. The question that arises is why will more people prefer a system that has no legal backing and fraught with inaccurate dataset to one that is legally compulsory based on scientifically accurate surveys and also claims to offer indefeasible title? The answer to this could dictate policy direction and reforms. Since costs are widely accepted as important disincentive to patronage, the ensuing section examines the respective cost implications of the two systems.

COSTS OF REAL ESTATE DOCUMENTATION REQUESTS

The official charges for one documentation under the plotting/concurrence system stood at about a third (¢300,000.00) of the cost of the land title system, which is ¢950,000.00. The study found that almost as a convention, in addition to the official charges, actors who request for documentation make extra official payments to staff of the responsible agencies to get their requests serviced as early as possible. Table 7 shows the detail extra-official costs incurred under both systems. Column 1 of the Table indicates the respective milestone activities available under both the land title and plotting/concurrence systems. To compute the costs, the costs per milestone activity were first estimated from the data obtained from the field survey. The costs per documentation procedure were then estimated by accumulating the costs of all the respective activities required to service particular requests for documentation under the respective systems. Thus, columns 3-10 are the costs of the different strands of processes used to service requests for the different forms of documentation under the registration systems.

Column 10 reports the unit costs incurred to have the documentation request serviced under the land title registration system.

The data show that the extra official costs incurred in having documentation requests serviced under the respective strands of procedures under the plotting/concurrence system range from a minimum of about £3,837.00 to a maximum of about £3,900.00 with an average costs of about £3,870.00. This is practically similar to the £3,860.00 under the land title system (see Column 10, row 19). Thus, the extra-official payments do not appear to have provided any significant incentive for the market to prefer one system to the other. Perhaps the differences in the official charges rather could explain the differences in the patronage between the two systems. This by itself does not tell much about the costliness of the system. Indeed it could even be cheap if the benefits from the documentation to the individual actors exceed these costs. Economic theory suggests, however, that if that is the case, utility maximising actors would be willing, subject to affordability, to bear the costs in order to receive the benefits. This means that overall requests for documentation will be very high if the benefits exceed these costs. However, given the reality that only 8% of potential requests for documentation have been made, it leaves no one in doubt that these costs hardly commensurate with the benefits that actors are gaining from the documentation. But how much is it costing the system to capture this information?

COSTS OF SERVICING DOCUMENTATION REQUESTS

The cost estimates for the respective processes are based on the labour hours spent per processing tasks as obtained from the field survey. Available direct labour hours are used as the allocation base to apportion the overhead costs (see Table 8 below).

In this analysis the total overheads are assumed to be the total budgets of the respective agencies less their personnel expenses. This approach assumes that the greater the direct labour hours for a task, the greater will be the overhead expenditure incurred. This may not necessarily be the case but offers a reasonable basis for apportioning the overheads and sufficient for the purpose of this study. To accomplish this, a single overhead rate for the respective agencies based on their staff numbers and approved budgets for 2008 is estimated. The estimates are reported in Table 10. The overhead rates are assigned to all processes handled by the corresponding agencies. Based on these, the costs for the respective task are established. Column 1 of Table 9 above is a break down of the policy processes into the major identifiable activities. The estimated labour and overhead costs for each of the activities together with their total costs have also been estimated in columns 3, 4, and 5 respectively. It could be observed that a conservative mark-up of 15 percent (see column 6) has been applied as provision for the incidents of costs that could not be established. The last two columns provide the equivalent costs in US Dollars and Pounds for ease of international comparison. Table 10 shows basically that the overall mean activity costs is ¢1,275,153 (Min = 72,523 and Max = 4,658,838, St. Deviation = ¢1,379,787).

Table 7. Non-Official Compliance Costs Grouped by Policy Processes

		State Lease Renewal	Concurrence	Stool Consent	Plotting	Allocation	State Consent	Regularization	Land Title
	Compliance Activity	Distributive	Regulative	Regulative	Regulative	Distributive	Distributive	Redistributive	Regulative
1	Transaction Documents	-	123,000.00	123,000.00	123,000.00	-	-	123,000.00	123,000.00
2	Site plan	-	128,000.00	128,000.00	128,000.00	-	-	128,000.00	128,000.00
3	Concurrence	-	920,000.00	-	-	-	-	-	-
4	Stool Consent	-	-	541,000.00	-	-	-	-	-
5	Plotting	-	-	-	558,783.78	-	-	-	-
6	State Consent	-	-	-	-	-	687,704.92	-	-
7	Land Title	2,800,000.00	2,800,000.00	2,800,000.00	2,800,000.00	2,800,000.00	2,800,000.00	2,800,000.00	2,800,000.00
8	Oath of Proof	-	107,425.13	107,425.13	107,425.13	-	107,425.13	107,425.13	107,425.13
9	Tax Clearance Certificate	158,529.41	158,529.41	158,529.41	158,529.41	158,529.41	158,529.41	158,529.41	158,529.41
10	Stamp Duty	142,196.65	142,196.65	142,196.65	142,196.65	142,196.65	142,196.65	142,196.65	142,196.65
11	Travel Time	9,509,120.00	9,509,120.00	9,509,120.00	9,509,120.00	9,509,120.00	9,509,120.00	9,509,120.00	9,509,120.00
12	Transportation	18,899,120.00	18,899,120.00	18,899,120.00	18,899,120.00	18,899,120.00	18,899,120.00	18,899,120.00	18,899,120.00
13	Waiting Time	1,790,780.00	1,790,780.00	1,790,780.00	1,790,780.00	1,790,780.00	1,790,780.00	1,790,780.00	1,790,780.00
14	Delays	28,600,824.67	28,600,824.67	28,600,824.67	28,600,824.67	28,600,824.67	28,600,824.67	28,600,824.67	28,600,824.67
	Total (¢)	61,900,570.73	63,178,995.86	62,799,995.86	62,817,779.64	61,900,570.73	62,695,700.78	62,258,995.86	62,258,995.86
	Total ($)	6,796.68	6,937.05	6,895.44	6,897.39	6,796.68	6,883.99	6,836.04	6,836.04
	Total (£)	3,837.22	3,916.47	3,892.97	3,894.07	3,837.22	3,886.51	3,859.44	3,859.44

Source: Field Survey (2008).

Table 8. Overhead Labour Rate

Overheads	Lands Commission	Land Title Registry	Land Valuation Board	OASL	Survey Department
Administrative Expenses	¢6,133,170,000.00	¢2,000,000,000.00	¢1,800,000,000.00	¢5,431,000,000.00	¢2,531,200,000.00
Service Expenses	¢1,442,170,000.00	¢2,400,000,000.00	¢2,538,400,000.00	¢89,488,000,000.00	¢1,949,400,000.00
Investment Expense	¢12,676,170,000.00	¢3,200,000,000.00	¢1,100,000,000.00	¢60,826,000,000.00	¢4,689,400,000.00
Total Overheads	¢20,251,510,000.00	¢7,600,000,000.00	¢5,438,400,000.00	¢155,745,000,000.00	¢9,170,000,000.00
Labour Force	264	82	818	251	539
Available Labour Hours/Day	8	8	8	8	8
Number Of Days Per Year	260	260	260	260	260
Total Direct Labour Hours	549,120.00	170,560.00	1,701,440.00	522,080.00	1,121,120.00
Overhead Rate Per Direct Labour Hour	¢36,879.94	¢44,559.10	¢3,196.35	¢298,316.35	¢8,179.32
Overhead Rate Per Direct Labour Hour ($)	$4.01	$4.84	$0.35	$32.43	$0.89
Overhead Rate Per Direct Labour Hour (£)	GBP 2.11	GBP 2.55	GBP 0.18	GBP 17.07	GBP 0.47

Source: Field Survey (2008).

Table 9. Summary Costing of Information Capture

	Information Capture Process	Direct Labour Costs	Overheads	Total	15% Mark-Up Margin	Grand Total	Grand Total ($)	Grand Total (£)
1	Concurrence	226,064.86	522,440.00	748,504.86	112,275.73	860,780.59	93.56	49.24
2	Stool Land Consent	183,207.80	461,390.00	644,597.80	96,689.67	741,287.47	80.57	42.41
3	State Land Consent	458,004.23	723,386.53	1,181,390.76	177,208.61	1,358,599.38	147.67	77.72
4	Plotting	139,559.77	251,970.00	391,529.77	58,729.47	450,259.23	48.94	25.76
5	State Land Allocation	1,246,417.74	1,222,850.00	2,469,267.74	370,390.16	2,839,657.90	308.66	162.45
6	Stamp Duty	51,896.08	11,168.00	63,064.08	9,459.61	72,523.70	7.88	4.15
7	Tax Clearance Certificate	44,308.57	102,900.00	147,208.57	22,081.29	169,289.85	18.40	9.68
8	Land Title Lodgement	15,503.58	142,720.00	158,223.58	23,733.54	181,957.12	19.78	10.41
9	Certificate Preparation	38,298.23	347,434.00	385,732.23	57,859.83	443,592.06	48.22	25.38
10	Title Certification	52,033.87	164,574.00	216,607.87	32,491.18	249,099.05	27.08	14.25
11	Regularization	2,057,974.10	1,993,190.00	4,051,164.10	607,674.62	4,658,838.72	506.40	266.52
12	Parcel Plan	377,991.64	140,958.00	518,949.64	77,842.45	596,792.08	64.87	34.14
13	Cadastral	1,895,021.73	517,092.00	2,412,113.73	361,817.06	2,773,930.79	301.51	158.69
14	Renewal Lease	1,199,528.89	935,730.00	2,135,258.89	320,288.83	2,455,547.72	266.91	140.48

Source: Field Survey (2008).

To appreciate the full scale of the costs incurred by both the government and market dealers to have real estate market information captured in Ghana, the costs computed from both ends have been put together. This is presented in Table 10. The Table reports at the top row, the major individual policy activities and the corresponding policy category under which they fall. Details of their corresponding compliance and administrative costs are then computed and reported accordingly.

BUDGET SHARE

To examine the adequacy of the resources devoted to these systems, the budgets of the responsible organisations are examined. But in the absence of any universally agreed standard for ascertaining the optimality of organisation's budgets, a comparative approach is adopted by which the budgets of these systems are compared with those of similar organisations. Rows 2 to 5 of Table 8 above show the average annual budgets of these agencies. Table 12 below presents an analysis of the share of these budgets on national internally generated revenue, tax and non-tax revenues. The computed proportion of the budgets on the total government revenue (column 6) is an index of the respective year's budgets' share of national revenue.

As reported in Table 12, the land sector's budget share of the preceding year's government revenue oscillates between a minimum of 0.25 percent in 2001 to a maximum of 0.65 percent attained in 2000. This works out to an overall average of less than 0.5 percent (Mean = 0.49%) share of government internally generated revenue in the corresponding preceding years.

Table 10. Descriptive Statistics on Costs of Processing Activities

	Direct Labour Costs	Overheads	Total	15% Margin	Grand Total
Mean	570,415.08	538,414.47	1,108,829.54	166,324.43	1,275,153.98
Min	15,503.58	11,168.00	63,064.08	9,459.61	72,523.70
Max	2,057,974.10	1,993,190.00	4,051,164.10	607,674.62	4,658,838.72
St. Deviation	719,477.83	542,361.56	1,199,815.38	179,972.31	1,379,787.69

Source: Field Survey (2008).

This diverges starkly from for, example, the forestry sector's average share of 1.5 percent (minimum = 0.04% and maximum = 2.42%).

Table 11. Aggregate Marginal Costs of Real Estate Policy in Ghana

Policy Process	State Lease Renewal	Concurrence	Stool Consent	Plotting	Allocation	State Consent	Regularization	Land Title
Policy Category	Distributive	Regulative	Regulative	Regulative	Distributive	Distributive	Redistributive	Regulative
Compliance Costs	61,900,570.73	75,178,995.86	74,799,995.86	62,817,779.64	61,900,570.73	62,695,700.78	62,258,995.86	62,258,995.86
Administration Costs	5,235,478.15	3,960,999.84	3,841,506.73	4,000,737.73	5,939,877.16	4,458,818.64	7,759,057.98	3,100,219.26
Total (¢)	67,136,048.88	79,139,995.70	78,641,502.59	66,818,517.37	67,840,447.89	67,154,519.42	70,018,053.84	65,359,215.12
Total ($)	7,297.40	8,602.17	8,547.99	7,262.88	7,373.96	7,299.40	7,610.66	7,104.26
Total (£)	1,533.09	2,219.82	2,191.30	1,514.93	1,573.39	1,534.15	1,697.97	1,431.44

Source: Field Survey (2008).

This is so even though the two agencies perform similar functions, the land sector focusing on the land side, which constitutes about 62.9 percent of the total land area and the forestry sector focusing on forestlands, savannah land transactions, shrub and thickets, which constitutes just about 26.6 percent of the total land area of Ghana (FAO, 2004). It does not, therefore, appear that the land sector is at least heavily resourced.

SIZE OF PERSONNEL ROSTER

In general, wages and salaries in the public services in Ghana are very low ,indeed lowest in West Africa (United Nations, 2002, p. 9). According to the World Bank (2005, p. 2) public service wage bill as a proportion of Ghana's GDP is lower than the average of low and middle-income countries. That said, a look at the empirical evidence from a comparative perspective shows that the land sector in practice deploys very small workforce in real estate market information capture in Ghana. The evidence as analyzed in Table 13 shows actually that the workforce sizes of the responsible bureaucracies are shrinking in real terms.

Overall, the agencies involved in real estate market information capture together employ a total of 1,954 staff across the 10 regions of the country, which is less than 0.3 percent (0.24%) of the total public service workforce of 800,000.00 (United Nations, 2005). The distribution of this total staff level among the individual agencies is even more revealing. Currently the Lands Commission, the agency responsible for the plotting/concurrence and deed registration systems has a total workforce of 264, an average of 26.4 staff per region and 0.03% of the public service. The Survey Department, which also services the land title system with all its survey map needs, has a workforce of 539, an average of 53.9 staff per regional office and 0.07% of the public service. The Land Title Registry, the agency responsible for the land title system has 82 staff (representing 0.01% of the public service).

If it is taken that each staff works for 269 days in a year and 7 hours in a day then the land title registry deploys a total of 154,406 man-hours per annum. Given that the Land Title registry receives on the average 7,452 applications per year (see above), it follows that 21 man-hours is required to complete an application (approx 7 man hours for 0.33 documentation service). Thus, with the existing strength, the registry should be servicing documentation requests at a rate of 28 documents per day, which appears reasonable.

Table 12. Comparison with Government Revenue (Million of Cedis)

Year	National Non-Tax Revenue	National Tax Revenue	Total Internally Generated Revenue	Subsequent Year's Budget for the Sampled Land Sector Agencies		Budget Share of Government Revenue (%)	
				Land Sector	Forestry Sector	Land Sector	Forestry Sector
1999	310,400.00	3,089,100.00	3,399,500.00	20,762.90	1,343.00	0.61	0.04
2000	961,600.00	3,731,700.00	4,693,300.00	30,596.10	74,883.00	0.65	1.60
2001	3,731,700.00	6,556,900.00	10,288,600.00	25,998.50	141,861.00	0.25	1.38
2002	252,400.00	8,547,500.00	8,799,900.00	42,029.10	212,585.00	0.48	2.42
2003	298,600.00	12,556,300.00	12,854,900.00	66,240.40	286,510.00	0.52	2.23
2004	1,136,300.00	17,403,000.00	18,539,300.00	76,652.60	251,122.00	0.41	1.35
Mean	1,115,166.67	8,647,416.67	9,762,583.33	43,713.27	161,384.00	0.49	1.50

Source: Data on non-tax and tax revenue were extracted from the budget statements of Ghana (1999 – 2005).

Yet the current average rate of 1178 per year (Table 2) implies that the registry is on the contrary delivering at about 4 documents per day. This explains a bulk of the delays. This does not appear to be the result of inadequate staff but inefficient or under employment of available staff. The absolute manual processing system employed in servicing requests worsens this. The situation is practically the same with the plotting/concurrence and deed registration systems under the Lands Commission.

Table 13. Real Estate Sector Workforce

		2001				2005			
Agency	Professionals	Sub-professional	Others	Total	Professionals	Sub-professional	Others	Total	Inter-census Percentage Change
Lands Commission	52	24	211	287	39	16	209	264	-8.01
Survey Department	33	29	459	521	33	35	471	539	3.45
OASL	23	21	205	249	23	21	301	251	0.80
Land Title Registry	7	3	56	66	23	36	23	82	24.24
Land Valuation Board	36	28	773	837	35	655	128	818	-2.27
Total	151	105	1,704	1960	153	763	1,132	1,954	-0.31
Percentage	7.70	5.36	86.94	100.00	7.83	39.05	57.93	100.00	

Source: Field Survey (2008).

Chapter 5

IMPLICATIONS

Figure 1 illustrates the implications of the preceding analyses. In Fig 1, take the vertical axis to represent the price of particular category of real estate; say real estate class *X,* while the horizontal axis indicates the likely quantities associated with particular prices. Take D_0 to denote the social optimal demand function for class *X* real estate under conditions of costless, perfect and equally distributed information. At this position, the equilibrium or optimal quantities of class *X* property expected to be purchased will be Q_0 at unit price $P_{0.}$

This price and quantity arrangements represent informed purchasers decision points and it will be the point at which the real estate market will be said to be performing most efficiently. Typically, few if any, real estate markets, like other specialists markets operate, as mentioned earlier, at this level owing to general paucity of information in pristine real estate markets. As Senior (1854; cited in Rose, 2002) argues “the detail of commerce are so numerous, the difficulty of obtaining early and accurate information is so great, and the facts themselves are so constantly changing that the most cautious merchants are often forced to act upon very doubtful premises”. This is even more so in the developing world where as Geertz (1978, p. 29) asserts: “information is poor, scarce, mal-distributed, inefficiently communicated and intensely valued”. This is not different from what actually pertains in Ghana, with only 8% real estate market information capture, huge backlogs of documentation requests to clear and inordinate inaccuracies in the records system.

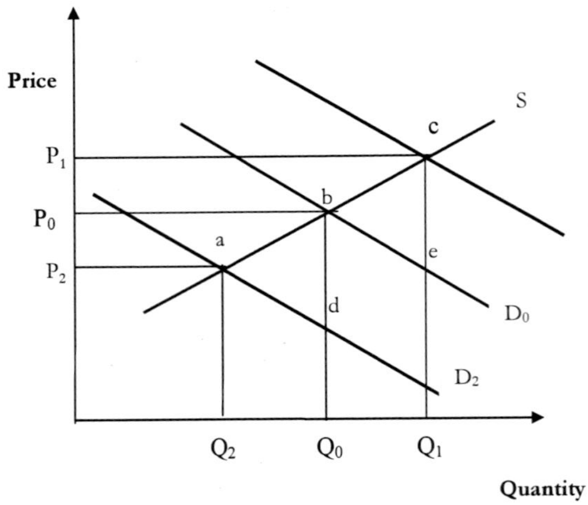

Figure 1. The Dynamics of Asymmetric Property Information.

The implications for Ghana can be daunting. As Akerlof (1970), Spence (1973), Rothschild & Stiglitz (1976) and Stiglitz (2001) have found, in such a system because real estate owners tend to know more about their properties including the quality of their titles than potential buyers or lenders, if purchasers proceed on the basis of their less than full and accurate information, multiple equilibriums could result. These may comprise one in which purchasers/lenders overvalue the intrinsic qualities of the real estate and the other in which they under value the intrinsic qualities. Much of the traditional literature on information asymmetry cited above focused almost exclusively on the scenario in which purchasers under-value the intrinsic qualities of commodities. The deeper implications of the scenario in which purchasers overvalue the commodity have has little attention in the literature and this is, thus, explored in this chapter.

If the intrinsic qualities of properties are overvalued, purchasers could bid higher or lenders could grant higher credit more than their actual optimal price. This means that instead of operating along D_0, such purchasers or lenders could, in fact, operate on a sub-optimal level D_1. At this level, Q_1 instead of Q_0 quantities of say class *X* real estate will be demanded at unit price of P_1. The practical consequences of the D_1 scenario are that real estate or land resources in this category will more likely be allocated to uses above their optimal capacity. This will lead to an efficiency loss as real estate is presumably taken out of its current use to a new use that will produce returns that are less than the price (P_1) offered for the real estate. For example, if residential real estate is overpriced to the levels of commercial real estate, the optimal returns produced by the particular real estate will match the optimal (P_0) for residential real estate (not for commercial real estate) and will most likely fall below those of commercial real estate say P_1. This premature allocation to commercial use may not be sustainable and could result in under utilization or inefficient use of the real estate at the expense of its actual optimal use, which is residential. From the credit market standpoint, real estate owners whose real estate is overvalued by credit institutions will have less incentive to pay up their loans as the amount of loan granted is likely to be much higher than the true price of the real estate. They, therefore, stand to gain more if they fail to pay up their loans.

These situations will most likely impose on society a social cost or deadweight loss represented by the triangle *bce* in Figure 1 on each unit of class *X* real estate acquired at price P_1. Motivated by the higher windfall returns or rent associated with overpricing, real estate owners are likely to firstly ensure that the rent associated with overpricing persists and secondly that where possible they grow by hyping the utilities of their real estate and downplaying the defects in their real estate to compel purchasers to overprice their bid and operate along D_1. Essentially, this is accomplished by withholding information, for instance, regarding defects in their real estate. This requires the expenditure of real resources to provide such information blockade through, for instance, the preparation and dissemination of false or misleading boundary maps and documents, the employment of personnel to peddle misinformation and even to maintain some form of physical presence on the land or real estate in the form of land guards among others.

These expenditures are incurred by diverting resources away from other productive sectors or uses just to prevent accurate information from getting to purchasers with the sole aim of maintaining a sub-optimal condition D_1. Indeed, if real estate owners do not protect this rent and, hence, overpricing, they can be sure that other suppliers (erstwhile purchasers who have now gained the true position of the information and, thus, realise they can gain by operating as suppliers) will attempt to enter the market and increase supply thereby forcing prices downward towards P_0. This shows that under conditions that lead to D_1 scenario the market does not provide appropriate incentives for information disclosure by real estate owners as their profits are maximised by the asymmetry and hence without any exogenous interventions, the asymmetry will prevail.

Conversely, if purchasers or lenders undervalue the intrinsic qualities, they do so because they perceive real estate in general as potentially problematic either as a result of title defects or otherwise. The result is that even high quality real estate in terms of title perfections, for instance, will also be priced the same as low quality ones by purchasers and creditors. This will lead to D_2 scenario at lower quantity Q_2 and price P_2. As Akerlof (1970) demonstrates, when this happens, high quality real estate owners will have no incentive to put their real estate on the market and hence most high quality real estate will be withdrawn leaving only problematic real estate on the market.

Nonetheless, on occasions, circumstances such as urgent need for money and other emergencies could force owners of high quality real estate to put their real estate on the market for sale. But then, real estate owners in bringing their real estate onto the market will prefer to supply their real estate between Q_2 and Q_0 in their existing uses because the returns from that use (discounted over time) as given by the area under the supply curve (abQ_2Q_0) exceed the price that is available in the market. This leads automatically to efficiency losses as these uses fall short of the optimal uses and hence the real estate is denied its highest and best uses.

If, however, purchasers fail to pay this price, then hard-pressed real estate owners will be compelled to sell their real estate at the price of a low quality real estate. In that case, it is this high quality real estate owner who eventually bears most of the inefficiency costs of the asymmetric information since all they may get for their real estate is the price of a low quality or defective registered real estate. The end result is that the real estate is more likely to be allocated to uses below their current capacity and would generate less returns than they should at the expense of the realisation of the social optimal for the society. The only actors who stand to gain in this scenario are the purchasers as they make savings on price but this again imposes social costs or deadweight losses represented on Figure 1 as triangle *abd* for each unit of real estate purchase on society. As a result, in this scenario, good quality real estate owners have the incentive to disclose their information to purchasers or lenders so that they could get better price for their real estate.

What emerges from this analysis is that: (a) real estate information asymmetry fundamentally leads to market distortions; and (b) all forms of market distortions result in social costs or efficiency losses. These social costs or efficiency losses arise out of a loss of producer surplus (the area between the supply curve and P_0 because some real estate owners would be willing to sell some quantity of real estate at a price between P_2 and P_0, and of consumer surplus (the area between P_0 and the demand curve D_1) as some buyers would be willing to pay more than P_0 for some of the real estate. In the long run, unless prevented by artificial barriers such as government interventions and legal impediments, economic theory suggests that the market will devise its own solutions to overcome the asymmetries. Spence (1973) drawing on insights from Akerlof (1971) shows that as a market solution, purchasers and lenders will most likely employ *signalling* to overcome the asymmetries by devising proxies or signals that will enable them approximate the key qualities of real estate they intend to deal in.

In Ghana, the pragmatic market signals used by purchasers in particular to ascertain the general title quality of real estate includes: (1) the ability of the owner to physically be in possession of the real estate as evidenced by the construction of permanent fencing, substantial development of the land and the owners' ability to deposit building materials on the site without fear of confrontation; (2) the regular presence of an onsite caretaker; and (3) positive testimonial from neighbours among others. Some purchasers and lenders rely on these signals to sort out or screen real estate owners. Particular purchasers or lenders would have their own predetermined threshold signal levels they require to be sufficiently confident to progress with the transaction and would sort out real estate sellers or borrowers as either being above or below the threshold level.

However, these have limited appeal to official purchasers or lenders, as they tend not to provide all the details that such transactions require including title defects. Yet equipped with the knowledge that some purchasers and informal lenders would rely on these signals, real estate owners have the incentive to incur signalling and other costs by again diverting resources from other productive sectors to acquire or put the relevant signals in place to attract purchasers. Rothschild & Stiglitz (1976) also show that in addition to signalling or as an alternative to it, purchasers and lenders may employ screening by offering a menu of questions or terms and relying on the choices made by real estate owners or borrowers to screen and categorize them into high quality or low quality real estate. In Ghana, screening is used more in addition to than as an alternative to signalling in real estate transactions.

Beyond the signalling and screening, private economic agents are also expected to emerge to take advantage of the accompanying arbitrage opportunity created by the asymmetry. Indeed, the work of real estate brokers, valuers, agents and solicitors among others is precisely to specialise in the acquisition and supply of this withheld accurate information to get the market going not at D_1 or D_2 but at D_0.

Where in particular society's private actors are sluggish in stepping in to supply the requisite information, which is what tends to be the case in the developing world, then government intervention may have to be invoked to bridge the information gaps and get the market going at D_0.

Chapter 6

CONCLUSION

The huge backlog of outstanding real estate ownership documentation in Ghana is perhaps the most crucial bane on the development of that country's real estate market. Any attempts at relieving that market of its inefficiency must necessary involve measures that will speed up the rate of information capture and remedy the inaccuracies in the system. The current arrangement as well as the proposed arrangements under the Land Administration Project (costing $53 million and funded by international donor agencies like the World Bank), does not hold the capacity to achieve this. The proposed arrangements are not different in essence from the system that has led to this situation. The most likely way forward would be a systematic real estate ownership census throughout the country to be financed by the state.

REFERENCES

Abdulai, R. T. (2007). The Operation of Urban Traditional Landholding Institutions in sub-Saharan Africa: A Ghana Study, Unpublished PhD Thesis, University of Wolverhampton, UK.

Abdulai, R. T. (2006). Is Land title regsitartion the answer to insecure and uncertain property rights in sub-Saharan Africa? RICS Research Paper Series, 6(6).

Abdulai, R. T. & Hammond, F. N. (2008). *Foreword, Real Estate and Development Economics Research Journal,* 1(1), pp.vi-ix.

Akerlof, G. A. (1970). The Market for 'Lemons': *Quality Uncertainty and the Market, Mechanism, Quarterly Journal of Economics,* 3, 488-500.

Alchian, A. A. (1965). *Some Economics of Property Rights, Politico,* 30, 816-829.

Alden-Wiley, L. (2002). Comments on the Legal Basis of for Land Administration in an African Context, Paper presented at the World Bank Regional Land Policy Workshop, Kampala, Uganda, 29 April - 2 May

AMCAD, (1998). Land Records Storage and Management Study, Accra: Ministry of Lands and Forestry, Government of Ghana and The American Cadastre Inc.

Antwi, A. Y. (2000). Urban Land Markets in sub-Saharan Africa: A Quantitative Study of Accra, Ghana, Unpublished PhD Thesis, Napier University, UK.

British Property Federation (BPF), (2006). Property Development and the Community: What are the Hidden Benefits of Development? Publication of BPF.

Brobbey, W. K. (1991). Improving Land Delivery Systems for Shelter, Final Report of Land Policy Consultancy, Accra: Government of Ghana, UNDP and HABITAT.

Chen, S. & Ravallion, M. (2008). The Developing World is Poorer than We Thought, But No Less Successful in the Fight Against Poverty, World Bank Policy Research Working Paper No. 4703.

Coase, R. H. (1960). The Problem of Social Cost, *Journal of Law and Economics,* 3, 1-44.

Cook, R. C. (2002). Alternative dispute resolution systems: what kind of alternative to the courts? *Paper presented at a Workshop on Land Rights and Legal Institutions in Kumasi* - Ghana, 28 Feb.

Council of Mortgage Lenders (CML), (2008). CML News and Views, Available at: www.cml.org.uk.

Deininger, K. (2003). Land Policies for Growth and Poverty Reduction, World Bank Policy Research Report, Washington DC and Oxford: World Bank and Oxford University Press.

Demsetz, H. (1967). Towards a Theory of Property Rights, American Economic Review, 57, 347-359.

De Soto, H. (2000). The Mystery of Capital: Why Capitalism Triumphs in the West and fails everywhere else. London: Bantam Press.

Feder, G. & Feeney, D. (1991). Land Tenure and Property Rights: Theory and Implications for Development Policy, The World Bank Economic Review, 5, 135-153.

Friedman, L. S. (2002). The Microeconomics of Public Policy Analysis. Oxforshire: Princeton University Press.

Geertz, C. (1978). The Bazaar Economy: Information and Search in Peasant Marketing, American Economic Review, 68, 28-32.

Goldsmith, A. A. (1995). Democracy, Property Rights and Economic Growth, *Journal of Development Studies,* 32(2), 157-174.

Hale, D. (2008). The Global Driver: How Housing is Drving the World Economy, Gale: Cengage Learning.

Hammond, F. N. (2006). The Economic Impacts of sub-Saharan Africa Urban Real Estate Policies, Unpublished PhD Thesis, University of Wolverhampton, UK.

Harberger, A. C. (1959). Monopoly and Resource Allocation, American Economic Review, 49, 134-146.

Hicks, J. R. (1939). The Foundations of Welfare Economics, *The Economic Journal,* 49(196), 696-712.

HM Land Registry (2009). 'Know where you stand – register your land', available at: www1. landregistry. gov. uk/ register_ dev/voluntary/

Ikejiofor, U. (2006). Equity in informal land delivery: Insights from Enugu, Nigeria, Land Use Policy, 23(4), 448-459.

MacKenzie, J. A. & Phillips, M. (2008). Textbook on land law. Oxford: Oxford University Press.

Mirrlees, J. A. (1971). An Exploration in the Theory of Optimum Income Taxation, Review of Economic Studies, 38(114), 175-208.

Nell, E. J. (1984). Free Market Conservatism: A Critique of Theory and Practice. Australia: George Allen and Unwin Publishers Ltd.

North, D. & Thomas, R. (1973). The Rise of the Western World. Cambridge: Cambridge University Press.

Pejovich, S. (1990). The Economics of Property Rights: Towards a Theory of Comparative Systems. Netherlands: Kluwer Academic Publishers.

Rao, P. K. (2003). The Economics of Transaction Costs: Theory, Methods and Application. New York: Palgrave Macmillan.

Rothschild, M. & Stiglitz, J. E. (1976). Equilibrium in Competitive Insurance Markets: An Essay on the Economics of Imperfect Information, *Quarterly Journal of Economics,* 90, 626-649.

Rose, M. (2002). Implications of Costly Information. Library of Economics and Liberty. Available at http:// econlib. org/ library/ columns/Teachers/ Information.html.

Rosenberg, N. & Birdszell, L. E. (1986). How the West Grew Rich: The Economic Transformation of the Western World, London: I. B. Tauris and Co Ltd. Publishers.

Senior, N. W. (1854). Political Economy. London: Richard Griffin and Co.

Smith, A. (1776). An Inquiry into the Nature and Causes of the Wealth of Nations. In E. Cannan, (Ed.), *Library of Economics and Liberty.* London: Methuen and Co., Ltd.

Spence, M. (1973). *Job Market Signalling, Quarterly Journal of Economics,* 87(3), 355-374.

Stigler, G. J. (1961). Economics of Information, *Journal of Political Economy,* 69, 213-225.

Stiglitz, J. E. (2001). Information and the Change in the Paradigm in Economics, Prize Lecture delivered at Columbia Business School, Columbia University, 8 December.

Torstensson, J. (1994). Property Rights and Economic Growth - *An Empirical Study,* Kyklos, 47(2), 231-247.

United Nations (UN) Department of Economic and Social Affairs (DESA) The Division for Public Economics and Public Administration (DPEPA), (2002). Report on the National Dissemination Workshop on

Public Service Ethics in Africa: The Ghana Country Report. New York: United Nations.

United Nations, (2005). World Population Prospects: The 2004 Revision, Highlights, New York: United Nations.

Vickrey, W. (1961). Counterspeculation, Auctions and Competitive Sealed Tenders, J. Finance, 16, 8-37.

Weiner, D. L. & Vining, A. R. (1999). Policy Analysis: Concepts and Practice (3 ed.). New Jersey: Prentice-Hall, Inc.

Williamson, I. (1991). Land Information Management at the World Bank, The Australian Surveyor, 36.

Williamson, O. E. (1981). Contract Analysis: The Transaction Costs Approach. In P. Burrows, & C. G. Veljanovski, (Eds.), The Economic Approach to Law. London: Butterworths.

Word Bank, (2007). Doing Business in 2007, How to Reform. Washington DC: World Bank and International Finance Corporation.

Wyatt, P. & Fisher, P. (1998). Property Information Today: Geographic and Land Information Management. In P. Wyatt and P. Fisher, (Eds.), Property information today: Geographic and land information management. London: Butterworths.

INDEX